In grateful appreciation

to our contributing poets

who, in the midst of

the clamor of life,

have helped to

bring peace and joy

to our many readers.

Salesian Missions wishes to extend special thanks and gratitude to our generous poet friends and to the publishers who have given us permission to reprint material included in this book. Every effort has been made to give proper acknowledgments. Any omissions or errors are deeply regretted, and the publisher, upon notification, will be pleased to make the necessary corrections in subsequent editions.

Poems of Joy

from the
Salesian Collection

Compiled and Edited
by Sara Tarascio

Illustrated by
Paul Scully,
Frank Massa
and
Russell Bushée

CONTENTS

Pathway Gifts

Have you ever taken notice -
As you walk your earthen ways -
Of the pleasures, God has scattered
On our paths of night and day:
       Pretty flowers - in abundance;
       Trees of majesty and might;
       Golden strands of playful moonbeams
       Chasing shadows, through the night?

And the smiles of joy and rapture -
That He graced on every road -
Have you ever taken notice
How they lighten weary loads:
       Fragrant fields of blooming clover;
       Laughing brooks and bubbling springs;
       Barren pastures, dressed in ermine;
       Painted songbirds, on the wing?

These are gifts that He has scattered
On the pathways of our time
To be treasured - like His blessings -
And a joy to humankind,
But we must take note - to see them -
As we walk our different ways
Or, forever, be the travelers
Seeing, only, dirt and clay.

Michael Dubina

Butterfly Day

I saw a butterfly today,
The color of the sun,
It made the garden dance for joy,
The flowers, every one --
It chased the wind's bright, fairy lips,
It hovered near a tree,
Sometimes it seemed the butterfly
Was writing poems for me.

I saw a butterfly today,
A jewel shining bright,
It shook my world's kaleidoscope
With patterns of sunlight,
I wish the summertime would last,
So that the butterfly could stay,
But I know that is just a dream --
And both will fly away.

Marion Schoeberlein

Never Alone

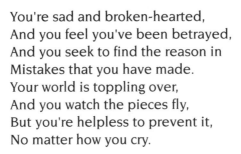

You're sad and broken-hearted,
And you feel you've been betrayed,
And you seek to find the reason in
Mistakes that you have made.
Your world is toppling over,
And you watch the pieces fly,
But you're helpless to prevent it,
No matter how you cry.

No man who ever lived has strength
Enough to stand alone,
And everything we have today,
Tomorrow may be gone.
So that is why no matter what,
Take care what you're about,
No happiness can ever come
From shutting Jesus out.

Each of us learns from failure,
To rise each time we fall,
This is the only way that life
Makes any sense at all.
It takes a lot of straining,
To walk that extra mile,
But nothing's free, we have to work
For everything worthwhile.

So do not weep for yesterday,
That you cannot recall,
And know within your heart, the Lord
Is with you through it all.
Though human love is here today,
And in a moment gone . . .
Who loves the Lord will always find
. . . He never walks alone.

Grace E. Easley

Song of the Bluebird

High on a windy hill
sits a bluebird, ever so still.
Iridescent in sunshine's rays,
he appears to be reverent. He prays.

There is something about him that says,
I am different. I have special ways
of surviving amidst the world's strife.
I have chosen a much higher life.

Then, from his throat comes a song
like none other I've heard my life long.
The tones are so pure and so sweet,
like a flute or an oboe, replete...

...with glory and wisdom and love --
a song from our Father above.
This bluebird is special to me.
From him, I have learned to be free.

Nancy Neff Dostie

10

As Day Begins!

The night is waning, Savior mine,
    Another day begins;
Oh would that I, this very day,
    A soul to Thee might win!

Oh would that I, this very day,
    Enrich another's life;
That those now shrouded in despair
    Be brought to Thee, dear Christ!

Oh would that I, this bright new day
    Might touch another's heart;
That I might share Thy light with one
    Now struggling in the dark!

For what is life without Thee Lord
    But just an empty sham;
And how can we observe our way
    Without Thy strengthening hand?

For Savior, tho' I older grow
    Oh may I not despair;
But rather, may my heart rejoice
    Because I've loved and shared!

Sancie Earman King

"Thou shalt love
the Lord thy God
with all thy strength,
and thy neighbor
as thyself."
Luke 10:27

The Meadow

Sometimes in the summer
I like to go
Down to the meadow
Where bright flowers grow.

I love all the colors,
And their fragrance so sweet,
And feel the cool grass
On the soles of my feet.

There's a small grassy knoll
On which I can lie,
And watch all the birds
As they go flying by.

A path which I follow
Down to its end
Leads to a brook
Just around the bend.

It makes a nice sound
As it babbles along,
Playing the melody
For the meadowlark's song.

Sometimes there are butterflies
With wings bright and shiny,
And all sorts of creatures,
Some ever so tiny.

Here I spend many hours
Close to Old Mother Nature,
And give thanks to God,
Such a wonderful Creator.

Olive B. Elvin

A Quiet Place

I often seek a quiet place
where weeping willows nod,
Where I can leave the world behind
and seek the voice of God.

I dare not speak while I am there
for this is holy ground,
And yet God hears my silent prayer
and there's no need for sound.

I feel the sun upon my face,
the wind upon my hair,
And He who holds the stars in place
renews my spirit there.

I hear the trickle of the stream,
the buzzing of the bee,
And I'm awake throughout the dream
that He reveals to me.

My senses let me know He's there,
unseen—yet face to face,
Bound by faith and love and prayer
in my holy, quiet place.

Clay Harrison

*"The words of wise
men are heard
in quiet..."*
Eccl. 9:17

Simple Sounds

How sweet the gentle sounds of life!
   A creaky rocking chair,
The rattle of a teacup,
      are so pleasant to my ear.

How dear the sounds of morning
      when the paper hits the door,
And the children's tinkling laughter
      as they run across the floor.

These simple sounds of living
      are the notes and melody
Of the lovely background music
      for my dearest memories.

                    Frankie Davis Oviatt

14

Candles of Hope...

Candles of hope are burning bright
From the dewy morn till the dusky night;
Candles of hope are burning clear,
And we see their lovely vision near...

Candles of faith are burning free,
And their glow is soft for you and me;
Candles of faith are burning true,
And their light is strong for me and you...

Candles of joy are burning bright
From the early morn till the starry night;
Candles of joy are burning free,
And they speak of love and ecstasy!

Hope C. Oberhelman

No man, when he lights a
candle covers it, but sets
it on a candlestick so
that who enter might
see the light.
Luke 8:16

To Walk With Humility

Give me faith and child-like trust
To follow in the path I must;
For things unseen are in Thy hands.
Thy love and grace forever stands
    'twixt ill and me.
Whatever be the day's raw mold,
I know for sure, the hours hold
In confidence, that good that comes
    from knowing Thee.
The world is large, the heavens great:
With angels and with men, I trust and wait.

Roxie Lusk Smith

Happiness

I sought the path to happiness
Through power, wealth and fame,
Yet everything that I possessed
Appeared to be in vain.
Nothing seemed to satisfy
Or elate my restless soul
While I kept reaching for the sky
For that desired goal;
Then unexpectedly, I found
A tome, its pages old,
With a message most profound
In illuminated gold.
"Love thy neighbor as thyself,
Have faith and charity,
And a cheerful merry heart,
If happy thou wouldst be."

Elsie Natalie Brady

The Voices of the Sea

In sounds of surf on wind-swept shore,
    A rhythmic rhapsody
Of music stirs my heart to hear
    The voices of the sea.

Softly, like a whisper, they
    Will often speak to me
Of spacious worlds as yet unseen,
    Beyond all land and sea.

My heart beats wild, for swiftly flows
    The constant ebbing tide,
And swiftly, too, life's rhythmic sea,
    And voices soon subside.

A poet's dream? Perhaps, yet I
    Am sure they speak to me.
When all is hushed and still, I hear...
    The voices of the sea.

Sister Miriam Barker

Beauty in All

Every sea-shell is not perfect
Though in each some beauty can we see;
So it is with family and friends
Who are dear to you and me.

A beautiful spot of color shows through
When we look beyond imperfection;
When we're willing to accept the ugly spot
Our lives take a new direction.

When we can see all as God sees us
And look past the faults of others,
Only then will we be ready
To join all nations as Christian brothers.

Helen Kitchell Evans

*…He that loveth God
loveth his brother also.*
1 John 4:21

Golden Flowers

Golden flowers in October,
In a field around the bend,
Twining in and out of fences,
Waving grandly in the wind.
Planted by a loving Master,
Tended by His gentle hand,
Pause awhile and see the beauty,
He has spread across the land.

Golden flowers bright with sunlight,
Growing four and five feet tall,
With their dark brown button centers,
Are the crown jewels of the Fall.
Never could an earthy artist,
Duplicate their vibrant hue,
Perfect in the smallest detail,
As they sparkle in the dew.

And my heart is filled with wonder,
That my lips cannot express,
And my eyes are wet with tears
Because I feel such happiness.
And I know God lives within me,
In the beauty of it all,
In this bird's eye view of Heaven,
Down a country road, in Fall.

Grace E. Easley

This is the day which the Lord
hath made; rejoice and be glad.
Ps. 118:24

20

Almighty God, we offer thanks
to You upon this day,
For all the blessings You have brought
In Your most wondrous way.
> We thank You for the flowers and trees
> In all their colors bright;
> The dawning of each new born day,
> The solitude of night.

Dear God, we thank You for the rain
And too the sunshine bright;
The birds that sing upon the wing,
An always welcome sight.
> We thank You for the wondrous work
> Created by Your hand,
> That makes this land in which we live
> So beautiful and grand.

We thank You, God, with humble hearts
For all You give and do.
Each thing of beauty on this earth
Reflects a part of You.

Harold F. Mohn

*Give thanks to the Lord,
for He is good, His
mercy endures for ever.
1 Chr. 16:34*

A Prayerful Day

Each morning as I wake up
and face a brand new day,
I pause for just a moment,
and take the time to pray.

I thank God for safe-keeping
of my family through the night,
and for the brand new morning
that's so beautiful and bright.

I thank Him for my blessings,
and for what He has in store;
For altho' He's done so much for me,
I know He'll do much more.

And then I ask for guidance,
so that I can find my way.
For without Him I would stumble,
and with temptations surely stray.

Then as the day comes to an end,
and nighttime closes in,
I pause for just a moment -
and talk to God again.

Diana Sue Lindley

Rules for Daily Living

Begin the day with God;
    Kneel down to Him in prayer,
Lift up thy heart to His abode
    And seek His love to share.

Open the Book of God,
    And read a portion there,
That it may hallow all thy thoughts,
    And sweeten all thy care.

Go through the day with God,
    Whate'er thy work may be,
Where'er thou art — at home, abroad,
    He still is near to thee.

Converse in mind with God,
    Thy spirit heavenward raise,
Acknowledge every good bestowed,
    And offer grateful praise.

Conclude the day with God,
    Thy sins to Him confess,
Trust in the Lord's atoning blood,
    And plead His righteousness.

Lie down at night with God,
    Who gives His servants sleep,
And shouldst thou tread the vale of death,
    He will thee guard and keep.

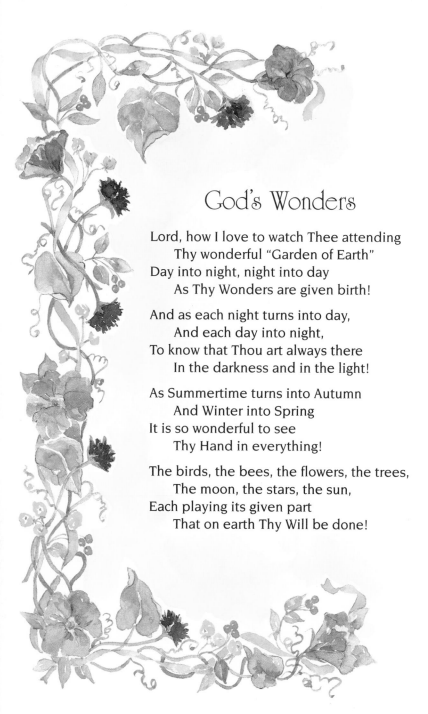

God's Wonders

Lord, how I love to watch Thee attending
 Thy wonderful "Garden of Earth"
Day into night, night into day
 As Thy Wonders are given birth!

And as each night turns into day,
 And each day into night,
To know that Thou art always there
 In the darkness and in the light!

As Summertime turns into Autumn
 And Winter into Spring
It is so wonderful to see
 Thy Hand in everything!

The birds, the bees, the flowers, the trees,
 The moon, the stars, the sun,
Each playing its given part
 That on earth Thy Will be done!

Snow and rain, thunder and lightning,
    Cold and heat, all given
By Thee, to make so wonderful
    This "Garden of Eden" we live in!

And even in these wonders
    Thou art calling unto man
To see Thy Power and Glory
    That we come to trust in Thy Hand!

So that we might be able to do this
    Thou didst give Thy Son Jesus Christ
That whosoever believes in Him
    Shall have everlasting Life!

That we might dwell in Heaven with Him,
    A place Christ went to prepare,
And far surpassing this "Garden of Earth"
    Will be the Glory we'll find there!

No pain, no tears, no sorrow,
    But joy and praise forevermore
For all who accepted, while on earth,
    Jesus Christ as their Saviour and Lord!

Ruth V. Eaker

Bless Caring Hearts

Lord, bless the hearts of those who care
For others every day...
The ones who to the helpless souls
Are bright and shiny rays.

Bless the ones who minister
With ready, out-stretched hands
To every wearied traveler
Upon this pilgrim land.

Lord, bless the hands and feet of those
Who tend to all in need...
The shut-ins and the many folk
Who live upon the streets.

Oh, bless the Good Samaritan
Who sacrifices self,
Who always goes the extra mile
To help somebody else.

Loise Pinkerton Fritz

For the Season a Time

This morning at daybreak,
I looked at the sky,
Today would be cloudy
The "weather not dry"
The season is winter,
But, then yesterday,
It seemed that the springtime
Had melted away
All traces of chill
That called winter weather,
But today would be rain
And would bring stormy weather.

I pondered a while
Then I wondered aloud,
Why one should feel blue
Just because of a cloud,
For a cloud has a purpose,
And holds beauty you know,
For there must be rain
So the flowers will grow,
It's part of God's plan
When the earth He designed,
For the rain there's a reason,
And the season, a time.

Katherine Smith Matheney

*To everything
there is a season,
and a time to every purpose
under heaven.*
Eccl. 3:1

27

We Gain Strength

Life is composed of experiences,
Some both good and bad,
When we fall and hurt ourselves,
We shouldn't stay down and sad.

Life is an "uphill" battle,
There's no way to "breeze" through,
 Just how well we handle it,
Is up to me and you.

There are some things that we do,
For a while seem negative,
Never think of them as that,
They teach us how to live.

Like in youth, the little boy,
Who fell and scraped his knee,
We learn from every time we fall,
It teaches us to heed.

'Cause every time we fall and hurt,
The struggle to our feet,
Overcoming these afflictions,
Makes us strong—not weak!

We must be optimistic,
Each event a stepping stone,
The Lord will help us through it,
So we never are alone.

For He knows we're not perfect,
Mistakes we're bound to make,
What we need is fortitude,
He gives us strength to take.

So never feel guilty,
About experiences you've had,
They all turn into positives,
We improve and should be glad.

Those who never err and fall,
Simply remain the same,
It's only those who take a chance,
Who have everything to gain.

Hope Ulch Brown

James Ross

Just Around The Bend

I'm getting near the summit now,
  Close to my journey's end;
And looking back, I thank Thee God,
  For all that Thou didst send!

For every stormy wind that blew
  Across my changing way;
For faith that held me in its clasp,
  Secure both night and day;

For valleys deep I had to cross,
  Some hard to understand,
But none so rough but I could feel
  The pressure of Thy hand;

For bright plateaus of peace, where I
  Could pause to rest awhile,
To worship, and to gain new strength
  To climb another mile;

For golden opportunities
  To share this priceless treasure
Of Thy dear love with other hearts –
  That joy no scale can measure!

I know not how far it is
  Before my journey's end,
But I think I hear the harps of God –
  Just around the bend.

Alice Hanche Mortenson

Open Up Your Heart

Count the grains of sand. How many?
See the distant star. How far?
Drops of water in the ocean…
That's how loved you are.

Overflowing… growing, growing,
more and more and more.
Cup is filling, cup is spilling.
Love is running o'er.

Everywhere is God's abundance.
Look about and see.
Pick the fruit. It's ripe!
It's ready! Come, partake. It's free!

See it, see it, all about you.
Will you do your part?
God is ready, how about you?
Open up your heart.

Dolores Dahl

Brightening Light

There's a light that grows and brightens
With the passing of each day,
That will bring me resurrection
From a lifetime of dismay;
It will light - again - the splendors
Of a world, my sins resigned,
And will loose the chains of anguish
That enslave my heart and mind.

I will walk - again - its pastures
And its paths of happy days
And I'll find - again - its pleasures
And the joys I've cast away;
Every love of heart and fondness
I'll pursue, to reap anew -
With the Lord to be my Shepherd
And a guide to all I do.

Michael Dubina

*To give light
to those that
sit in darkness,
to guide our
feet into the
way of peace.*
Luke 1:79

Happiness is Little Things

Happiness is little things,
A book, a cup of tea,
A card or letter in the mail,
Especially for me.

To see a rosebush in full bloom,
Be warmed by glowing sun;
To snuggle in a cozy bed
When the day is done.

A good night's rest, a brand new day,
The warmth of friendly hand;
A note, a smile, a touch, a hug,
Someone to understand.

Days of hope and hours of love,
Savoring each minute;
Happiness is in your heart
If thankfulness is in it.

Viola Jacobson Berg

Suitable for Framing

Each day You paint a picture, Lord
    As the sun begins to rise,
And we see there on Your canvas
    A sight that thrills our eyes.
And then You take Your palette, Lord,
    And paint each budding rose
And sprinkle them with butterflies
    Before the sunlight goes.
At twilight time You come again
    To paint a masterpiece
As the gnomes of daily living
    Surrender to Your peace.
By night You paint with tongues of fire
    Across the darkened sky
A memory so amazing
    That it shall never die.
Each day You paint a picture, Lord,
    For everyone to see
Each suitable for framing
    In the halls of memory.

Clay Harrison

The Glory of His Crown

Life can often bring us burdens
that are difficult to bear,
And so many times a heartache
that no one else can share;
Though the joys we know, too often,
are outbalanced by our woes -
Yet I gladly bear the briers
for the beauty of the rose.

Though it's good to feel the sunshine
and to walk within its light
We would never see the stars
if there were no such thing as night,
And a sky ablaze with diamonds
is a sight beyond compare -
And I gladly bear the darkness
just to see them shining there.

Though the upward climb be weary
and the pathway strewn with stones,
And you often feel like quitting
for the aching in your bones,

Though each weary step be painful
and your mind keeps crying "stop" -
Yet I gladly bear the struggle
for the vista from the top.

Love that walks away from trouble
is a worthless love indeed,
And a faith that shrinks from testing
may be just an empty creed,
But the faith that meets and conquers
owns the Earth from pole to pole -
And I gladly bear the trials
that lend stature to my soul.

Duty's path is always rougher
than just going with the crowd,
While Her voice is sometimes muffled,
pleasure's call is clear and loud;
Though the road where Jesus points me
I may tremble to go down
Yet His cross I'll gladly carry -
for the glory of His crown.

                              Alban Wall

You Have Done It Unto Me

If you helped someone in need today
If you eased some pain along the way
Befriending one who went astray
Jesus said, "You have done it unto Me."

If you fed the hungry, clothed the poor
If you helped the handicapped endure
And made the lonely feel secure
Jesus said, "You have done it unto Me."

If you helped someone who had to bear
Heavy burdens, suffering and care
And kept that person in your prayer
Jesus said, "You have done it unto Me."

If you answered a stranger's pleas
For assistance through life's stormy seas
You've helped one of the least of these
Jesus said, "You have done it unto Me."

John and Edna Massimilla

*What you have done unto the
least of my brethren, you
have done it unto Me.*
Matthew 25:40

38

Little Things

Love is doing little things
Remembrance is the joy it brings.
It lends a warmth to every heart
Little things are so great a part
Of what it's like to love the best
To run the mile and pass the test.
God doesn't ask you to be the lark
Or brighten skies with your spark.
He only asks what you can do
To plod along 'til you are through.
Your labors need not be so fine,
But quiet, soft and quite benign.
Hardly noticed by the like of these
But greater far than forest trees.
Because they sought no great reward
But merely to help others toward
Some sheltered love which is from God.
Doing little things isn't very hard.

Jean Quigley

Our Time Together

Lord, when the sun is turning all
The morning sky bright pink,
It's such a special time for me
To take the time to think
Of all the things that make Your world
A lovely place to be:
Good health, a smile to share with all,
And friends, and family.
I love to spend this peaceful time
With You, my dearest friend,
Who knows my secrets and my dreams
And helps my heart to mend.
So as You paint the world each morn,
This blissful time we'll share,
Close by my window to the world
Here in my rocking chair.

Sandra Town Lytle

*In the morning I will direct
my prayer to Thee, and look up.*
Ps. 5:3

Enjoy Today

Enjoy today, it will not come again,
Waste not the hours thinking of tomorrow,
More than half our heartache and our sorrow
Are over what the future may contain.
The darkest doubts and worries never changed
The color of the sky nor turned the tide,
But he whose faith burns like a light inside,
Questions not the things God has arranged.
"For everything a season," every man
Must journey from the old to reach the new,
Discovering as he is passing through
The desert, an oasis in the sand.
For there are dreams that really do come true,
. . . And this is all we need to understand.

Grace E. Easley

It Only Takes A Moment

It only takes a moment
  to do a thoughtful thing.
Just think of all the happiness
  our thoughtful acts might bring.
Why, it only takes a moment
  to pick up the telephone
And say hello to someone
  who is sitting home alone.
And it only takes a moment,
  when someone is feeling blue,
To send a cheery little card
  or pen a line or two.
It will only take a moment
  to extend a helping hand
Or give someone assurance
  that we really understand.

And it only takes a moment
    from our busy working day
To say a prayer for someone,
    be they near or far away.
"But I can't, for I'm too busy…
    I just haven't got the time";
How often have we said it,
    like an old familiar rhyme.
Yet each moment is God-given,
    every one a treasure rare,
Not to be hoarded selfishly
    but meant for us to share
In our little acts of kindness,
    words that cheer and comfort bring,
For it only takes a moment
    to do a thoughtful thing.

                Alice J. Christianson

The flowers appear on the earth;
the time of the singing of birds has come.

Song 2:12

Journey Through The Years

Walking down life's rambling pathway
On this journey through the years,
Sometimes joyful hearts are singing,
Often crying lonely tears.

Born upon a bed of caring
To a mother's loving arms,
Father's gentle hand to guide us
Sweet protection from all harm.

Flowers all along our pathway,
On this journey through the years,
But the curving road before us
Often hides much pain and tears.

Yet we need not fear the future
Even though it is unknown,
For we have a loving Father
And He watches o'er His own.

Even when our days of sunshine
Turn to storm clouds and to rain,
We can always find a rainbow
And new courage to sustain.

So whatever fate awaits us,
On this pathway through the years,
When life's journey here is over,
God will wipe away our tears.

Gertrude B. McClain

Dreams Do Come True

Tap into the Tree of Life
And you will surely find
A warmth there to embrace you
Of an everlasting kind.

For once you feel His presence
Oh, how glorious life will be
For you will leave behind a shadow
Of the you... you used to be.

A new today will greet you
For you have turned around
And tapped into the Tree of Life
Now a "new you" has been found.

Now blest in rich abundance
And crowned with jewels unseen
Oh, how miraculous the discovery
When we take the time to dream.

Chris Zambernard

Autumn Prayer

The gold of all the world today
Cannot compare with that which lay
      about my feet.
A brisk, cool autumn wind came by
      and felt complete.
She gave up all her golden store
Which fell and lay upon earth's floor
      (Her yearly feat).
Aladdin's lamp could conjure up
No over-flowing brim to sup
      that is so sweet.
The riches that the Master sends
Which lay about my feet transcends
      all else. To treat
Us briefly with the Midas touch
For which we mortals yearn so much
      I stand complete.

                Lavonne Childers Minigh

Autumn's Promise

Falling leaves of terra-cotta scatter
in the breeze...
Amber hues and tawny shadows covering
the trees...
Billowing puffs of azure float across
the sky...
In shapes of cotton sculptures ever-
changing to the eye.
Squirrels bury their stolen acorn
treasures...
While birds hurry toward the sun's
warm pleasures.
Autumn holds the promise of 'His'
return to earth...
The season of harvest that renews itself
in springtime with rebirth!

Georgene Freedman

Give Me A Share Of These

Give me the sun of October skies
And the beautiful breaking dawn,
The afternoon with its sweet surprise
And the twilight when day has gone,
Give me the thrill of an autumn rain
With its lingering gentle breeze,
The silver glow of the stars again
Give me a share of these.

Give me the splendor of autumn's gold
And a field that is turning brown,
The million colors so bright and bold
In the leaves that are falling down,
Beauties of nature throughout each day
That after October is past,
I'll have a mem'ry to put away
That forever will live and last.

Give me October, just as it is
With anything it might bring,
From a frosty morn to an evening's bliss
And an autumn day between,
At peace with the world, in a woodland still
Neath God's ever beautiful trees,
A valley below that looks high up a hill
Give me a share of these.

Garnett Ann Schultz

The Rarest of Gifts

Every day is a reason
for giving, and giving
is the key to living...
So let us give "ourselves" away
Not just today but every day...
And remember a kind
and thoughtful deed
Or a hand outstretched
in time of need
Is the rarest of gifts,
for it is a part
Not of the purse but a loving heart –
And he who gives
of himself
will find
True joy of heart
and peace of mind.

Helen Steiner Rice

Used with permission of
The Helen Steiner Rice Foundation
Cincinnati, OH 45202

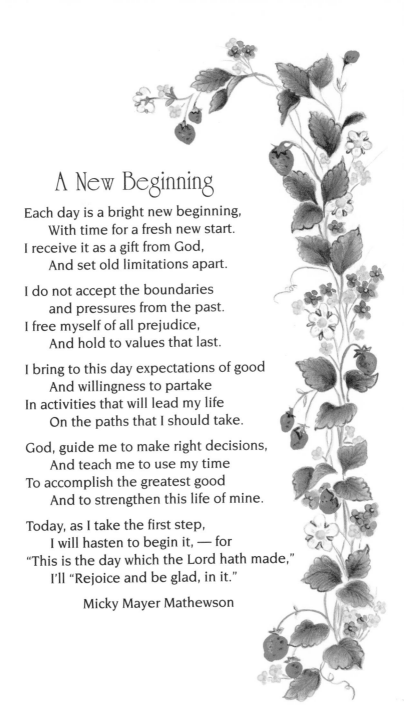

A New Beginning

Each day is a bright new beginning,
    With time for a fresh new start.
I receive it as a gift from God,
    And set old limitations apart.

I do not accept the boundaries
    and pressures from the past.
I free myself of all prejudice,
    And hold to values that last.

I bring to this day expectations of good
    And willingness to partake
In activities that will lead my life
    On the paths that I should take.

God, guide me to make right decisions,
    And teach me to use my time
To accomplish the greatest good
    And to strengthen this life of mine.

Today, as I take the first step,
    I will hasten to begin it, — for
"This is the day which the Lord hath made,"
    I'll "Rejoice and be glad, in it."

          Micky Mayer Mathewson

Present Tense

A tiny seed
asleep in the dark earth,
awakening to produce
a lovely flower…
The buried root
winding up through
the cold ground,
sending out
new shoots…
The bare tree
lifting leafless branches
toward the gray-washed sky,
anticipating promise
and fulfillment…

God breathes into
the heart of all things:
Life has its time
of being.

Though I may possess
a winter heart,
Lord, give me that springtime
growth
and renewal.

Roxie Lusk Smith

*"For in Him we live, and move,
and have our being; as certain
of your own poets have said…"*
Acts 17:28

Symbol of Love

There was a beautiful sunset,
    A rosy, glorious glow.
The promise of pleasant pastime,
    A time of refreshment to know.

Tomorrow I'll work in my garden,
    Omnipotently pull up a weed,
Stake drooping, heavy flowers,
    Give support where there is need.

I'll rejoice in the promise of harvest,
    Caring, planting is not in vain.
It takes some time, preparing the soil,
    But the harvest depends on the rain.

My garden is blessed and nurtured,
    Not by me, but by God above.
His gracious provision, life in a seed.
    My garden shows forth His great love.

Ruth C. Grace

Dance Softly to the Music

Dance softly to the music
    wafting gently down the years...
Let peace billow the pages
    against inner eyes and ears.

Touch tenderly the passing thoughts
    for they are butterflies;
Hours are only seconds
    and moments only sighs.

But silently the Hands of God
    are holding, stilled in light,
The timeless notes of memory
    like canvassed birds in flight.

And somehow all the sights and sounds
    and scent and taste and feel
Of the life we thought was gone are there,
    more precious, sweet and real.

Then, orchestrated well for me,
    is the song I cannot sing
But only know: That all of life
    is love and memory.

Frankie Davis Oviatt

Make Your Day

When your heart is heavy,
Lift it with a song,
A happy, lilting melody,
When everything is wrong,
Always in a major key,
Presto, forte, full of glee,
Raise your voice unstintingly,
Pour out joy wholeheartedly,
Scatter gloom and doom away,
A song will do it;
make your day.

Ruth Moyer Gilmour

O sing to the Lord a new song,
all the earth, and bless His name.
Psalms 96:1,2

The Rose Will Bloom Again

Lord, help me through this sorrow,
Take my worries and my woe;
I trust Your loving mercy,
For this I've come to know.

Sometimes I lack the courage
And the will to carry on;
I lose sight of the rainbow
With the absence of the dawn.

Lord, lead me to the sunlight,
Show the comfort of Your smile,
Let me feel life's soothing waters
As I walk with You the while.

Lift me from this darkened valley,
Take away this hurtful pain,
Giving sweet assurance that
The rose will bloom again.

Catherine Janssen Irwin

A Rose in November

Today out my window
I saw something there,
A rose in November,
So pretty and fair.
It's a blossom of splendor
Seemed touched from above
By the Master Who tended
With patience and love.

Its color of beauty
Is hard to describe.
The rose of November
Though cold, still alive.
Although not the season
For something so rare,
It stood at the corner
So lovely and fair.

"I think it's a symbol,"
I said to myself,
Like my neighbor who lives
In the little brick house,
For her friendship I cherish
Is so special and rare,
Like the rose in November
In God's own loving care.

Katherine Smith Matheney

A Little One

A little one should know of God
Of greening fields and upturned sod,
Where violets bloom in early spring
The kiss of sun and birds on wing,
To marvel at the blue of sky
And climb the hill that reaches high.

A little one should romp and play
And catch a sunbeam on the way,
To walk barefoot midst Junetime flowers
And be caressed by April showers,
To race the wind and laugh in fun
Delight where little streamlets run.

A little one should ever find
A lasting dream and peace of mind,
Where nature dwells - the treasured spot
A buttercup - forget-me-not,
Exploring fields and roaming free
A glimpse of shining majesty.

The meadows - woods - God's wondrous earth
To know and realize their worth,
Each growing thing - the hidden place
Where pansies show a smiling face,
A valley deep - a mountain tall
A little one should know it all.

Garnett Ann Schultz

58

I See Thy Glory, Lord

From the smallest flower to the tallest tree,
   I see Thy glory, Lord.
From the babbling brook to the mighty sea,
   Thy handiwork's explored.

From the morning sun to the stars at night,
   I see Thy glory, Lord.
From the winter snows to spring's delight,
   Thy name has been adored.

From the cotton fields to the western plains,
   I see Thy glory, Lord.
From the changing tides to the summer rains,
   Thy power can't be ignored.

From a mother's prayer to a baby's cry,
   I see Thy Glory, Lord.
From the ocean depths to the mountains high,
   Thy majesty's explored.

I see Thy glory, Lord, wherever I go –
   Thy power can't be ignored.
From heaven above to the earth below,
   I see Thy glory, Lord!

Clay Harrison

*The heavens declare the glory
of God; and the firmament
showeth His handiwork.*
Ps. 19:1

The Journey Back

Come with me upon a journey,
As I turn the old clock back,
There's a mighty engine roaring,
Down a million miles of track.
Now there isn't time for packing,
So we'll go the way we are,
I can see the black smoke rising,
So she can't be very far.

She was never one for stopping,
So we'll have to flag her down,
Grab that lantern in a hurry,
For she's at the edge of town.
And I wouldn't want to miss her,
'Cause she's part of yesterday,
And there's no one left to meet her,
When she passes back this way.

She is one with childhood's memories,
Grown sweeter with the years,
My best remembered lullaby,
...Her whistle in my ears.
So step aboard her platform,
I have my old pass, yet...
And take a journey back through time,
You never will forget.

Grace E. Easley

Gift of Dawn

Let your life begin, anew,
With each day that dawns for you;
Dream, again, your dreams of youth -
Kindle faith and hope and truth;
Let your spirits rise each 'morn
With the flowers that greet the dawn.

Life is always young and new,
When the earth is fresh with dew;
Birds awake to sing and fly;
Angels paint the eastern sky;
You are born again - this day -
To enjoy God's loving way.

But you must not waste this time -
Lost in folly or in wine -
For this day may be your last
To repent for sins of past.
You must finish deeds, begun -
Say and do what must be done.

Let this dawn fulfill your day
With the loves that bless your way.
See the joys of earth and sky,
You have scorned or hurried bye.
Let your life begin, anew,
With this dawn God gave to you.

Michael Dubina

Help thy brother's boat across,
and lo! thine own has
reached the shore.

Companion

When I went strolling on the shore
    Beside a turquoise sea,
Where palm trees swayed and dolphins played,
    God's love enveloped me.

And when I climbed to mountain peaks,
    I found His presence, too...
In meadowlands, on desert trails,
    Neath starlit skies of blue.

God walked with me through happy times,
    And on each rocky road;
His strength helped ease the burden of
    An extra-heavy load.

Though life may take me far and wide
    Until my journey's end,
I'll be at peace, for by my side
    Is God, my dearest friend.

                  Sandra Town Lytle

I'll Say A Prayer For You

When days are dark and dreary
And you don't know what to do
You're tired and oh so weary
I'll say a prayer for you.

When life seems full of sorrow
And the good things seem so few
'Twill better be tomorrow
I'll say a prayer for you.

When smiles are hard to come by
No matter what you do
Just look to God who sits on high
I'll say a prayer for you.

When you are lonely and despair
And no one's there with you
Remember God is always there
I'll say a prayer for you.

And when, each day, I kneel to pray
My thoughts will be of you
I'll ask your pain be wiped away
I'll say a prayer for you.

Ruth Sells

*Therefore I
will look unto
the Lord; my God
will hear me.*
Micah 7:7

God Loves Us

God loves us
This we know -
His beautiful world
Tells us so!

Flowers and fruits
and beautiful trees -
Majestic mountains
Lakes and seas.

Summer and winter,
Spring and fall -
He never fails
To bring them all!

Rivers that flow
Serenely along -
And birds that sing
Their own sweet song.

Soft fluffy white clouds,
In skies so blue -
And stars at night
Shining down on you.

A beautiful rainbow
When storms have ceased -
And new life to earth
The rains have released.

Oh yes, God loves us,
We surely must know -
Daily mercies and blessings
Really tell us so!

Helen S. Moore

Look at the birds: they do not plant seeds,
gather a harvest and put it in barns;
yet your Father in heaven takes care of them!
Aren't you worth much more than birds?
Matthew 6:26

Our Purpose

We have a purpose here on earth
That spans the passing years,
It goes beyond our daily needs
The laughter and the tears.

It goes beyond the earthly cares
And all the joys of living,
Beyond our loved ones and our friends
The taking and the giving.

It even goes beyond our church
The preaching and the praying,
The fellowship in one accord
The organ softly playing.

That purpose lies beyond our home
Our church and occupation,
Beyond the city where we live
Beyond our own dear nation.

We have a purpose for our lives
And things that we must do,
For there are sinners all around
That we must witness to.

We need to be a witness here
But that is just a part,
For sometimes people only hear
The message of the heart.

The heart that reaches out to man
To show a Savior's love,
Will make them feel His presence here
Not just somewhere above.

A kindly deed, a helping hand
His lovelight shining through,
A purpose for each child of God
Some service we must do.

Gertrude B. McClain

Wondering

I wonder that the flowers thrive
When planted in the sod,
And why the Father chose a cave
To house the Baby God.
I wonder that we can't behold
The wind that blows the trees
And why we cannot glimpse our God,
The Power in every breeze.
I wonder at God's mighty works,
His land and sky and sea
And marvel He has chosen me
To love eternally.

Sr. Mary Gemma Brunke

My Prayer

I pray for:
A little house by sand and tide
Where seashells on a shelf abide,
Enough to eat and some to share
With old and new friends who come there;
Enough to wear, a cozy fire,
A pillow soft when I retire.
Gratitude for simple pleasure
(A cup of tea, books and leisure),
A dog to snuggle at my feet,
Making my joy the more complete.
Good health that I may myself tend
And peace with God to be my end.

Marjorie S. Branson

Moments
Precious

One thing we often fail to do
is live a precious moment through.
Sometimes they swiftly pass away,
but others linger round for days.
Our problem is to recognize,
and then to grasp the precious prize.

How often was our patience thin
to some poor soul who was our friend.
And also did we so complain
when asked to help relieve some pain.
What final word, perhaps a sneer,
was last to pass a loved one's ear?

Too often moments pass us by
before we sense the loss inside.
How many of them have we had,
yet squandered in our push ahead?
O late we see our chance gone by
to heal a wound or soothe a cry.

O moments precious to us now,
would that we could relive somehow.
Yet they are gone, no more to come,
we had a chance but only one.
And Lord we humbly pray of Thee
that we may recognize and see
those moments that are yet to come.

William Marshall Weller

Dear Lord...

Let me treasure every hour
Of this very precious day...
Let me count my blessings many
As I wend my busy way...

Help me to be worthy
Of all the beauty nigh...
The trees and perfumed flowers
And cotton-tufted sky...

Make me aware of loveliness
Wherever it prevails...
Be it in a crowded city
Or on tranquil country trails...

For this day is oh, so special
And will never reappear...
So may I walk with gratitude
And each hour held most dear.

Virginia Borman Grimmer

71

At Peace With God And Man

I sat beside a summer stream
　　One lazy afternoon;
The stillness that pervaded there
　　Was like a sweet perfume.

I saw the wild grapes climb the trees,
　　I watched a dragonfly,
While dancing in the unkempt woods
　　Were sunbeams from on high.

I saw the sumac everywhere.
　　Like fireworks in bloom,
The cone-like flowers thrust through greens
　　And burst into scarlet plumes.

I saw a turtle swim the stream,
　　In thickets spied a hare;
A woodchuck, wandering carelessly,
　　Stopped briefly by my chair.

I sat beside a quiet stream
　　One summer afternoon;
At peace with God and man, I found
　　The world in perfect tune.

　　　　　　　　Loise Pinkerton Fritz

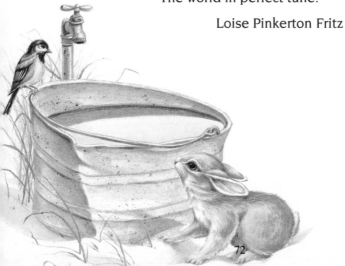

72

A Pack of Seeds

I bought myself a pack of seeds,
    To grace my garden fair,
And stuck them in my pocket.
    For months they waited there.

And when the time had come to see
    The flower's lovely face,
I thought it strange that only weeds
    Were growing in the place.

I bought the seed; I know I did;
    I even paid the price;
But still I don't have flowers
    To make my garden nice.

How foolish then, oh Christian man,
    God's Word, you have indeed.
You carry it or hide it
    But do not plant the seed.

No fruit there grows in garden fair,
    Unless the seed you sow.
For you the Word of God must plant,
    Then God will make it grow.

                Charles G. Ramsey

A Home...

...Is where there is warmth and love
 When blasts of ice and snow
Crash our skyward hopes and dreams
 Into ruins below.
And though some cold may penetrate
 round a sagging door;
Or clouds may cover up the sun
 Slanting across the floor;
Yet a home is the place where faith returns
 To pierce the deepest gloom;
Where kindness changes the atmosphere
 Of a frigid room.
It's a place where we are understood,
 Even as we are blind
To all the priceless values,
 Within our heart enshrined.

A home is the place where God is found
 Using the finest art;
As He brushes over the winter scene...
 And paints flowers in the heart.

    Vada Whitmore

Point of View

I've heard it said it all depends
Upon your point of view,
The happiness you get from life,
And how things look to you.
And the longer that I'm living,
I've really come to see,
That this is just as true a fact,
As anything could be.

If you always look for sorrow,
Then you'll have it seven-fold,
If you go in search of rainbows,
You will find a pot of gold.
If you have no time for dreaming,
The days are dark and grey,
But with a little bit of hope,
Your troubles slip away.

Don't waste your time in sighing,
When the world is full of song,
Don't live among the shadows,
That is not where you belong.
Lift your face and feel the sunlight,
Smell the flowers in the wood,
And be grateful you are living,
...And know that God is good.

Grace E. Easley

Keep Smiling

Keep smiling when the sun would hide,
    And shadows fall like night —
When storms would toss and turn you 'round,
    And nothing would be right.

Keep smiling, for the sun's around
    The corner, never fear—
For then the clouds will vanish, and
    The skies will soon be clear.

Keep smiling, 'tho your heart would break,
    And tempest take its toll —
When tears, like rain from angry skies
    Would flood your troubled soul.

Keep smiling, yes, for clouds will part,
    And sun will soon begin
To warm your heart as God restores
    Your peace and joy within.

            Sister Miriam Barker, C.D.S.

The Sea

The rugged coast where land meets sea,
In spite of the ocean's roar,
Has such a peaceful quality
As the foamy waves hit shore.

But the sea is made of many moods
It never keeps a rule -
Sometimes it seems quite playful,
At others rough and cruel.

When it is calm and peaceful
The waves just gently nudge
As if to say "come play with me,
I bear no one a grudge."

But when a storm is brewing
And its power pounds the sand,
The wild waves seem to be guided
By a strong, invisible hand.

I think perhaps the fury
Of the lashing, white-capped sea
Is a dramatic way to remind us,
Of a power much greater than we.

Dorothy Kohlberger

Lord thou art God, which has made
heaven and earth and the sea
and all that is in them.
Acts 4:24

Home Sweet Home

Lord, please bless our home sweet home,
Grant it love and cheer;
May the folks you bring to us
Feel your presence here.

Cast out thoughts of wrath and hate,
Cause all strife to cease;
Clear the air of fear and doubt,
Fill each room with peace.

If we stray from off the path,
Lead our steps aright;
Walk with us through each new day,
Hold us close at night.

May your angels watch o'er us
As we go down life's road;
Please make yourself at home, dear Lord,
Abide in our abode.

Connie Hinnen

*"Blessed be your coming
and blessed be your going."*
Deuteronomy 28:6

Mansions and Memories

Enjoy the treasures of your life
    That God has made to be,
And all the pleasures, loves and joys,
    You feel and hear and see,
For these are blessings willed to you -
    Upon your hour of birth -
And meant - for you - to share and sow
    Throughout your life on earth.

But mansions that you build in life
    You cannot ever own,
For you must leave them - every one -
    When God commands you Home -
And, in your place, some other souls
    Will live their life, in kind,
And live within the mansions
    You built and left behind.

But they must leave their mansions, too -
    When God exacts their soul;
And they must leave behind - as you -
    The treasures they extol,
For you can only take of life -
    To carry to your grave -
Your memories of life on earth
    And hopes for being saved.

                Michael Dubina

God's Handicrafts

I saw God at His work today
Creating flowers in bright array.
It is a wondrous thing to me
The grasp He has of chemistry.
Last week a single slender rod
Had thrust its head above the sod,
Soon followed by a host of stems
With buds on top, like diadems.
And then this morning blossoms came,
Some white as snow, some bright as flame.
No artisan or engineer
Can duplicate what I see here;
No painter's brush can match their skill,
These artists on my windowsill.
To one who thinks it common sense
To buttress faith with evidence,
These flowers say more without a word
Than all the sermons ever heard.
In this compact of sun and sod
I see the very hand of God;
Let fools maintain the argument
That it is merely "accident."

Alban Wall

The Tree

I love the tree behind my house,
Its quiet majesty -
A tribute to the Art of God -
Surveys eternity.

It moves in graceful pantomime
With every passing breeze,
While in its branches soft ballet
Is being danced by leaves.

It must have stood since time began
As, reaching for the sky
(Unchanging in its solemness),
The world is marching by.

I wonder what serenity
Within its strength abides -
While in its boughs and arching limbs,
Tiny creatures hide.

The tree has little brothers
By the stream not far away,
They're reeds that bend with blowing wind;
In every breeze, they sway.

A symbol of the hope of men,
The tree takes stubborn stand
Of goodness by the side of God,
Enduring till the end.

I want to be like this tall tree,
Enduring till the end,
And keep my faith that I won't sway
Like reeds in passing wind.

Frankie Davis Oviatt

The Potter

He's the God of the sunshine
And God of the rain.
He knows what to send us
Of gladness and pain.
For He is The Potter
And we are the clay.
He's patiently molding
Our lives every day.

Sometimes He sends blue skies,
And other times gray,
Then blends all together
In perfect array.
So we must not question
His plan or "delays,"
For great is His wisdom,
And best are His ways.

The Potter is working
In your life and mine
To make of us vessels
Through which His love shines.
Oh, may we stay yielded,
His will to obey
To come forth perfected
In His chosen way.

Beverly J. Anderson

Spring Will Come

It was sometime in the fall
And there behind the garden wall
The bulbs were spread like pods of gold
For their internment to the cold
And as I placed them in the ground
I wondered "will I be around
When Spring proclaims their glorious day?"
And underneath the bed of clay
Their life will all begin anew
In colors of the rainbows hue
With tulips dancing on a hill
Beside the golden daffodil.

I pondered on this mystery
The shriveled life I could not see
A mystery so sweet to tell
That far beneath our hidden shell
And covered by the winters past
There lives a seed, that when at last
The Spring will come, and then
I know, a new life will begin.

Margaret Loyd Rockwood

Reach Out

In everyone's life there comes a time
when our faith is put to the test,
and we feel that we're losing touch with God,
though we're doing our very best.

It may seem that the world is against us,
and there's no one around to care,
but if we just "reach out" we'll find
that God is always there.

If we let Him know that we need Him,
and our faith is very strong—
He'll wipe away the cares of the day,
and fill our hearts with His song.

For He is the light in the darkness,
our pillar to lean upon,
and He'll give us the strength and courage
we'll need to carry on.

Doris A. Orth

Come Quickly, Spring!

Come quickly, Spring, like an arrow's flight
And shatter winter's long, dark night.
Spring forth with buds upon each tree
With crimson skies above the sea.
Return the rose and the daffodil
And nesting birds upon the hill.
Return the babble to the brook
And the silver catfish to my hook.
Sprinkle stardust and pale moonlight
Throughout the jasmine-scented night,
And tune my ear to the buzz of bees
And hummingbirds in days like these.
Awaken me to golden skies
With singing birds and butterflies.
Fill my garden with a bright array
Of flowers for a grand bouquet.
Come quickly, Spring, to the earth below
And set my heart and soul aglow!

Clay Harrison

One Wintry Morning

One wintry morning long ago
When I was just a child
The silence was so calm and deep
'Round lovely snowdrifts piled.

With nose to glass I knelt and peered
Upon this sparkling world
Of sun and sky and purest white
Where nature's wings unfurled.

The doe appeared with gentle step
To pause at forest edge;
A squirrel sat to sniff the air
Close by the garden hedge.

I saw God's artwork everywhere
And marveled at the view
There as a child adoring life
When magic times were new.

                    Norma Childress

Just a Dog

Don't ever call him "just a dog"
    Who haven't the eyes to see,
That I belong to him as much
    As he belongs to me.
God must have had His reasons,
    For making the likes of him,
And I humbly hope with all my heart,
    …That I was one of them.

The years have dulled his russet coat,
    And his vision is getting dim,
And he walks with a limp when days are cold,
    'Cause the dampness gets to him.
He's not as young as he used to be,
    And his whiskers are frosted white,
But he wags his tail as if to say,
    "You see, I'm still alright."

I cut his food in bite-size chunks,
 And he gives me a toothless grin,
Trusting in my love for him,
 Whatever shape he's in.
He has accepted growing old,
 The way men cannot do…
And I'm not ashamed to say he's taught
 Me more than a thing or two.

So don't ever call him "just a dog"
 Unless you are prepared
To match his steadfast loyalty,
 To care the the way he's cared.
For many the sad offenses,
 Committed in Love's name,
And how many times it takes a dog
 …To put a man to shame!

Grace E. Easley

89

Homecoming

The blue of the sky is bluer today
Than it ever was before;
The song of the bird is sweeter still
As it sounds the village o'er.
The blossoms of pink on the orchard trees
Waft a fragrance of no-named perfume,
And the roses carpet the trellis high
With a cover of reddest bloom.

The little brown fence, encircling the yard,
Is leaning more beautiful still,
And the dusty old path trails a sweet-smelling dust
As it circles its way to the mill.
The wild flowers, tended by God alone,
Shed a beauty no garden has known…
No wealth can equal these joys untold
To a wanderer coming home.

Loise Pinkerton Fritz

90

Recipe for Happiness

Let not the western gates of day
    Close on the setting sun,
Let not a night of stars slip in
    Without a good deed done;
It might be just the smile you give
    To some poor weary soul
That would lift him from the shadows,
    And lead him to his goal;
It might be just the word you speak
    To a discouraged heart
That would be the power needed
    To give him a fresh start.

Our smiles are like the golden sun,
    Our deeds like silvery rain,
Our words, the seeds we scatter 'round
    That harvest joy or pain;
This is our mission here on earth
    If we live by God's plan,
To make our lives more beautiful
    We must help fellowman.

Dorothy M. Cahoon

Shells

When I hear the word "shell"
The thought comes to me,
of sunny bathed beaches
and shells by the sea,
tossed up by the waves
from the perilous deep,
intricate treasures
for mortals to keep!

However these shells
are only one kind.
There are many others,
observing, you'll find
there are shells around peanuts
and walnuts and wheat,
to be carefully opened
to find the real meat.

There are shells,
God forbid it,
to be shot from a gun,
fashioned by man,
not by God's Son.
There are shells around turtles,
with covers complete,
whenever from danger
he wants to retreat.

There also are shells
that we cannot see,
shells of withdrawal
to hide you and me,
from which we must break
that others may find
Joy in our sharing
God's love and His mind.

There's also the shell
of these bodies of clay
that will be transformed
in a moment someday.
In the meantime they cover
the most precious thing ---
our souls --- let us praise Him,
and may our hearts sing
with the joy of forgiveness
and cleansing from sin,
and that someday we'll live
forever with Him!

Alice Hansche Mortenson

To Trust in Thee

How can I say,
"Thou knowest best,"
When I am grieving
In the test?
How can I say,
"Thy way is right,"
When I am drained,
Too weak to fight?

O Lord, if I
Should challenged be,
Give me the faith
That trusts in Thee.
Let me go forth
From where I stand,
And leave the matter
In Thy hand.

Roxie Lusk Smith

Whate'er Befalls

'Tis not for me to question
The joys and woes of life,
'Tis not for me to ponder
Why there is stress and strife.
For I am frail and weak as dust,
But faith alone shall serve the just.

'Tis hard sometimes to understand
The world's aggressive greed;
The violence and injustice,
The poverty and the need...
Although these evils thrive and gain,
God's wisdom and His love remain.

His power and plan turn mystery
To certainty intense;
And questioning to affirmation,
Complaint to confidence,
The Lord is all the strength I know,
To Him all glory I bestow.

Felicia Sivagnanam

Lord, I Believe

Great wonders without number
does the mighty Lord my God!
He watches without slumber
o'er the rugged path I trod.
I do not see His glory
in a dazzling cloud of white,
but know His voice and story,
and I walk by faith, not sight.
If seeing is believing,
I believe He's truly there:
In gladness and in grieving,
He still answers every prayer.
I see His grand creation
of the sky and earth's attire.
I know love's transformation
by the Holy Spirit's fire,
and though I have not seen His face,
I know the greatness of His grace.

Patricia Kackman

Coffee Time

It matters not the time of day
The season or the weather
There's always time for coffee
When good friends get together.

I've found in many walks of life
Decisions are best made
If first you take a coffee break
And then the plans are laid.

You have a heated argument
And tempers want to burst?
Take ten or fifteen minutes —
Have a cup of coffee first!

You'll find that most all tempers
Will disappear quite fast
And when you do get back to work
Your differences have passed.

In fact, you may have reached the point
Where rather than offend
You'll find that you have taken time
To make another friend.

Beverly Enderby Kimzey

Precious Treasures

Precious treasures are yours and mine,
When we trust in Christ divine;
A home in Heaven awaits us there
Where there's no pain, grief, nor despair.

Untold pleasures and joys unknown
We'll receive from God's own throne,
And royal mansions for ev'ryone
Are promised us by God's dear Son.

And while we walk this earthly clime,
Heaven's grace is yours and mine
To give us strength whatever our task,
Until we're Home with Christ at last.

Earthly treasures can ne'er compare
To His love our Saviour shares,
While all our needs are filled by our Lord,
According to His blessed Word.

Love's rich treasures are yours and mine,
Christ's own life with ours entwined!
We'll never fathom such matchless grace,
Till we behold Him, face to face.

Kathryn Thorne Bowsher

The Master's Garden

Help me cultivate Thy garden;
Help me plant it, row by row;
Keep me sowing, gracious Master,
That every seed may thrive and grow...

Help me cultivate Thy garden;
Help me plant each precious seed;
Hope and faith and love and mercy—
All the things my soul doth need...

Help me cultivate Thy garden;
Blessed Master, stay Thou near;
Help me water it and watch it
As each seedling doth appear...

Help me cultivate Thy garden;
Keep me sowing, oh my Lord—
Help me labor in the garden
Where every flower is Thy reward!

Hope C. Oberhelman

Creation

God created the earth
    and the heavens above,
He mastered this task
    to show His great love!
He made day and night
    to work and to rest,
He spread dark and light
    from East to the West.

He divided the waters
    and filled them with food,
Brought forth living creatures,
    God said it was good!
He sculptured the mountains,
    He painted the skies,
He puffed-up the clouds,
    and made the sun rise.

He placed stars in the sky
    and gave them a glow,
He centered the moon
    to shine down below.
He breathed life into trees,
    gave fragrance to flowers,
He lowered the rainbows,
    and blessed all with showers!

The power to the seas
    He gave with great care,
In His Omnipotence
    compared it to prayer!
We need to explore
    the world's greatest worth
From the treasures He buried
    in the depth of the earth!

He labored six days
    when the projects were done,
He rested on the seventh,
    pleased with each one!
But His greatest achievement
    engineered to His plan,
Was when, in His Self-image
    He created...man!

        Hedwig Wroblewski

At Close of Day

As shadows are falling at the
    close of day,
I go to my garden to thank God
    and pray.
There's no place I feel closer to
    my Lord and my God
Than there midst the roses and
    green fragrant sod.
Sunset splashes its rosy pink
    hues
And night dims the sky's bright
    vivid blue.
I kneel down in wonder and
    fervently pray,
Thanking God for the blessings
    He sends us each day.
There's no place I feel closer
    to my Lord and my God
Than here in the garden midst
    the green fragrant sod.

Elizabeth B. Delea

God's Grace

There's a great, wide world around
  us
And an arc of sky above,
There are trees and flow'rs and
  sunbeams,
All are symbols of God's love.

There are clouds high in the
  heavens,
Big with promise of spring rain,
There are strong winds from the
  mountains,
Swirling, sweeping o'er the plain.

Brooks and rivers in the valley,
Hurry on their seaward way,
And the green grass of the
  meadows,
Is where newborn lambkins play.

Everything combines to tell us,
Of God's mercy and His grace,
Of His care and His provision
Given to the human race.

Lily S. Thomas

*The Lord will give
grace and glory*
Ps. 84:11

That Old Green House

That old green house where I was born,
Whose walls were bare and windows worn,
Was small in size, and didn't make
A picture that folks want to take.
It must have had three rooms at best,
And looked exactly like the rest,
But there I was the happiest,
    ...For it was home.

That old green house where I was born,
Had no bright flowers to adorn
Its tiny yard, but there was grass
Where I could play and watch folks pass.
And I am sure I can recall
One pretty picture on the wall,
And even small as I was small,
    ...I called it home.

That old green house where I was born,
May have been gazed upon with scorn,
For standing in a neighborhood,
Some people didn't think was good.
But it stood bravely, none-the-less,
Beneath its sagging roof, I guess
It felt the love it saw expressed,
    ...In such a home.

That old green house has long ago
Been gone from where it stood, I know,
But I am sure, on looking back,
It stood beside a railroad track.
And though I try, the years erase
The memory of Mama's face,
And after that... no other place
    ...Was ever home.

                    Grace E. Easley

Cathedral by the Sea

Lord, in the morning when I rise
    And throw the shutters wide,
Blithe sea gulls greet me at my door
    Beside the ebbing tide.

I love to smell the salty breeze
    As I rush toward the sea
To stroll upon the soothing shore,
    And start my day with Thee.

Could I but count each grain of sand,
    The sum could not compare
With all the times I've come to You
    For strength, in heartfelt prayer.

Each seashell is a token of
    An answer from above
That gave me strength to carry on,
    Enveloped in Your love.

Your care is constant as the waves;
    I'll trust eternally,
And daily give Thee thanks in my
    Cathedral by the sea.

             Sandra Town Lytle

Echoes of the Lord

From dawn to dawn; Through night and day -
No matter where we go -
We hear the echoes of the Lord
In all that He bestowed:

> In the laughter of our children;
> In the songs that people sing;
> In the breeze that plays in tree tops;
> In the fluttering of wings;
> In the mirth of rushing rivers;
> In an ocean's rhythmic flow;
> In His lightning strikes and thunder;
> In the hush of falling snow.

Everywhere - on land and water -
We can hear His echoes ring;
Everywhere are His reminders:
He is Lord of everything;
But His truest, finest echoes
Are in prayers we choose to say
And we echo - what He taught us -
When He taught us how to pray.

Michael Dubina

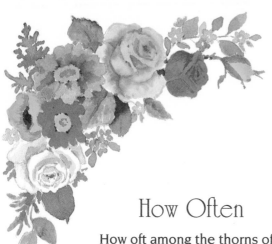

How Often

How oft among the thorns of life
We find a fragrant rose,
And, oh, the joy of freedom
In every wind that blows.

How often in a shower
Appears a big rainbow,
And the most triumphant happiness
Is in eyes aglow.

How often in the din and roar
Will come the strains of song,
And sometimes joyous laughter
Comes from out a busy throng.

From unexpected places
How often comes a smile
And often just a little word
Makes living worth the while.

How often peace comes after strife
As through the years we trod.
How often do we overlook
These things that come from God.

Hildreth L. Patch

A Bit Of Heaven

I savor all the wonder
That captivates the eye,
From the river in the valley
To the clouds that span the sky.

I harken to the songbird's trill,
The rippling of a stream,
Soft breezes rustling thru the trees,
And allow myself to dream.

As the fragrance of the flowers
Permeates the air,
My thoughts are elevated
To heights I know not where.

I drink in all the beauty
That one heart can hold
And store it in my memory,
To a later time unfold.

Gracious God in all His glory
Sends sweet blessings every day,
But surely sends a bit of Heaven
When He sends the month of May.

Catherine Janssen Irwin

The Seashore

I watch as the ocean
With thunderous roar
Carries its whitecaps
Rushing to shore.

Smooth, shiny pebbles
Along with bright shells
Sparkle with sunlight
Tossed by the swells.

Breakers come crashing
O'er both rocks and sand
In powerful meeting
Of ocean and land.

Sandpipers scurry
At the edge of the sea
While gannets and sea gulls
Soar so gracefully.

My heart also soaring
I gaze joyfully
Singing God's praises
For such majesty.

Courtney A. Crawford

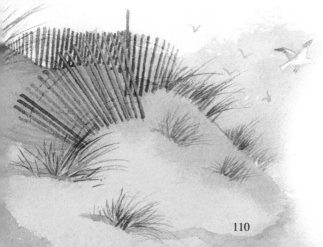

All Things Are Possible

I can move any mountain
   with God at my side.
I can weather the storm
   and drift with the tide.
I can hold out my hand
   for His hand is in mine.
I am never alone
   He's there all the time.

Friend you can move mountains
   with God at your side.
You can weather the storm
   and drift with the tide.
You can hold out your hand
   for His hand is in yours.
You are never alone
   for He is your source.

Helen Parker

*"If you have faith
you shall say to
this mountain 'move
from here to there' and
it shall move; and
nothing shall be impossible
to you"*
Matthew 17:20

I Count My Blessings

I count my blessings one by one
Though great or small they be,
And know without the help of God
Not one would ever be.

I thank Him for these blessings
Each morning of each day,
And then again at close of night
Before sleep comes my way.

He grants me all these blessings
Though sinner that I be,
And with the many faults of mine
I know that He loves me.

Harold F. Mohn

The Gift of Prayer

I'm sometimes so tired and weary
    That I can't seem to stand
For the road ahead is dreary
    Across life's burning sand.
It seems the nights grow longer
    When I can't see the light...
If my faith were only stronger,
    The path would be so bright.
Help me, Lord, to find the power
    To endure what lies ahead.
Be my guide every hour
    As I earn my daily bread.
Give me strength enough to rally
    Over hills I must climb...
Lead me through the peaceful valley;
    Lift me up one more time.
Be my friend when I am lonely;
    Be my refuge from the storm.
When I'm cold or lost or hungry,
    Take my heart and keep it warm.
Thank You, Lord, for being there,
    For loving me so much,
And thank You for the gift of prayer
    That keeps our hearts in touch.

Clay Harrison

Heavenly Gardener

How can I show my love for You --
Surely there must be ways,
Could I give my life to You,
Make a garden of my days?
I have not many more to give,
Dear Lord, You know that's true,
But every moment that I live,
I offer up to You...
I'd like to make my life a bower
Of flowers where You could walk
Along the pathway of my years;
Each day a flower on its stalk,
Each hour a petal of the flower,
Perfumed with fervent prayer
So You could see and smell and feel
My love as You walk there.
I know, dear Lord, (who'd know as well?)
They would not all be fair.
My faults, like blight and brown leaf curl
In ugly blotches would be there.
For these, I hang my head in shame!
Sin, like an ugly pest,
Sometimes disfigures flowers that should
Have turned out to be best...
But still - worm holes, leaf curl and all -
I give them up to You.
They're all I have to offer.
Just my life, until it's through.

Gertrude M. Carr

The Better Life

If worthy things in life could hold
    As deep and true a meaning
For us, as do the petty ones
    That take our time in scheming,
And all the other countless things
    Whose value is but seeming,
We all would live the better life
    Instead of dreaming... dreaming...

If we would tend our garden well,
    And watch the flowers growing,
We'd have less time to look across
    At what our neighbor's sowing.
And too, if we would guard our thoughts
    And find less fault with others,
I think we soon would criticize
    Ourselves, and not our brothers.

If we would truly rid our hearts
    Of envy, greed and pride,
And mend the trouble we have caused
    By sailing 'gainst the tide –
I think that we would soon forget
    The things that are so seeming,
And we would live the better life,
    Instead of dreaming... dreaming...

                Esther Nilsson

The Precious Name of Jesus

The precious name of Jesus
   the sweetest name of all
The name through which the Father
   receives my daily call.
The flowers of the field
   as lovely as they are
to such a name as Jesus
   cannot compare by far.

A name above all others
   this much I've come to know
I offer Him in earnest
   each prayer I utter low.
How much I love my Savior
   my lips may never tell
I seek in all Creation
   His presence therein dwell.

His name in all its splendor
   is written in the stars
All angels to His glory
   sing praises from afar
To praise His name forever
   they swell in one accord,
the precious name Jesus
   my Savior and my Lord.

              Thomas P. McHugh

I May Not See The Answer Now

He promised He would give to me
The things I need each day,
And I believe it in my heart
Each time I kneel to pray.

For when I call upon His name
And seek His face in prayer,
Through faith I see the answer is
Just waiting for me there.

I may not see the answer now
But still I must believe,
For He has never told a lie
And never will deceive.

He gives me everything I need
And even so much more,
My mind just cannot comprehend
The blessings left in store.

The answered prayer may not be "yes"
Or it may not be "no,"
And yet He answers for the best
Because He loves me so.

And He can see beyond this day
Just what is best for me,
So I must pray "Thy will be done"
And then wait patiently.

Gertrude B. McClain

Not to Seek, Lord, But to Share

Dear God, much too often
    we seek You in prayer
Because we are wallowing
    in our own self-despair...
We make every word
    we lamentingly speak
An imperative plea
    for whatever we seek...
We pray for ourselves
    and so seldom for others,
We're concerned with our problems
    and not with our brothers...
We seem to forget, Lord,
    that the "sweet hour of prayer"
Is not for self-seeking
    but to place in Your care
All the lost souls
    unloved and unknown
And to keep praying for them
    until they're Your own...
For it's never enough
    to seek God in prayer
With no thought of others
    who are lost in despair...
So teach us, dear God,
    that the power of prayer
Is made stronger by placing
    The world in Your care!

Helen Steiner Rice

Used with permission of
The Helen Steiner Rice Foundation
Cincinnati, OH 45202

Spring

Winter has shed its blanket;
The cold air is going away.
Nature is getting ready
For Spring to arrive any day.

The jonquils and tulips are blooming
And their fragrance is everywhere.
Spring has made its appearance;
You can feel it in the air!

We awake to a beautiful morn,
The sun splashing across our face.
Our steps are a lot springier
As we go to our appointed place.

Hearts seem to be more cheerful
As people go their merry way.
Ah! The splendor of the blossoms
And the beauty of the day.

It is a new awakening;
Dormant things are given new birth.
Winter has served its purpose
And Spring is now on the earth.

Dixie Gentry

Never Alone

When you feel alone and burdened
and it seems that no one cares,
there is One who walks beside you
and He tells you, "I'll be there."

Though the waters seem so troubled
and you cannot bear the pain,
you must never be discouraged,
there is sunshine after rain.

Often tears relieve the hurting
and you feel a sweet release,
as you give it all to Jesus
you receive a settled peace.

It is wrong to fear and worry
but we're human if we do,
in His perfect will He'll keep us
if to Him we're always true.

So in Him I feel assurance
there will come a brighter day,
if I trust upon His promise
daily read His word and pray!

Shirley McDonald

The Way
To Paradise

If you would find the path of life
Which leads to Paradise
Then heed the words our Savior spoke
And follow His advice.

Give unto others a helping hand
Aid to those in need
Conduct yourself as God commands
In thought and actual deed.

A friendly smile can help someone
Who thinks that no one cares
A thoughtful word can ease the pain
Of one in deep despair.

Give food to those who hunger
And drink to those who thirst
Visit the sad and lonely
And the sick who need a nurse.

Whatever you do for another
Whether a stranger or a friend
Will tilt the scales of justice
The day that this world ends.

God leads the way to Paradise
With love He sets the course
When He comes first in all you do
Then peace and joy are yours.

Dolores Karides

The Ultimate Surprise

My life is one big adventure!
Each day holds some new surprise...
Seeds sprouting in my garden,
A bird soaring in the skies…

The sudden view of a snow peak!
A small squirrel swishing his tail,
As we rest on our trek through the forest,
Wild violets beside the trail!

The arch of a lovely rainbow,
Through glistening drops of rain,
Or the pattern of wafting snowflakes,
And frost on my window pane!

An impetuous hug from a youngster,
The refreshing sparkle of youth,
Of innocent joyous laughter...
A smile with a missing tooth!

A gift, a phone-call, a visit,
On birthdays and holidays, too,
Looking through mail from the mailbox
And finding a letter from you!

Although my years have been many,
I'm beginning to realize,
I'll probably never get over
The joy of being surprised.

When my time comes to "go" I'll not mind it
This one last surprise, instead,
I'll tie a big bow on "Hereafter,"
And anticipate joy, ahead!

Micky Meyer Mathewson

A Home

A home is more than just a house
It's more than sturdy walls,
Or doors and windows shining bright
The stairways and the halls,
It's more than rooms we love so dear
A door thrown open wide,
For home is peace and gentle love
That lives and dwells inside.

A home is more than family ties
The treasured things we love,
Possessions that we fondly keep
A blue sky up above,
It's little ones laughing hearts
An understanding true,
The one spot in the whole wide world
Where hopes and dreams come true.

For home is everything worthwhile
It's heaven here on earth,
Contentment rich with happiness
The miracle of birth,
An ever understanding way
A gentle whispered prayer,
Protective arms to hold you tight
A home that dear ones share.

Garnett Ann Schultz

Because I Walk With God

Because I walk with faith in God
My life is far more bright.
Because I walk with faith in God
He is my guiding light.

Because I walk with faith in God
I have no sign of fear.
Because I walk with faith in God
His help is always near.

Because I walk with faith in God
He does my troubles share.
Because I walk with faith in God
I find Him everywhere.

Because I walk with faith in God
Each step along the way,
I find my life far more enriched
And more worthwhile each day.

                    Harold F. Mohn

Prayer Of Praise

Thank You for the golden rays
Of sun that turn our nights to days,
That warm the air, the streams, the sod,
And turn the wanderer back to God.

For melodies that fill the air,
The love and tenderness that come with Thy care;
For the golden hues and colors bright
That give us courage to walk in the night.

Thank You for friends so loyal and kind,
For loved ones dear, and peace of mind;
For a house of God to worship in,
But most of all for forgiveness of sin.

Thank You for the golden hours,
The days, the years, that bloom as flowers.
They weave a golden fleece to throw
To those we love where'er we go.

Father, this is my prayer of praise,
And may I never cease to raise
My voice in humble thanks to Thee
For Thy love so dear to me.

Grace Lee Frank Smith

A Beacon Light

I was drifting in the darkness
On the sea of dark despair,
Looking for a place of refuge,
I looked up and saw Him there.

From my wasted life of darkness,
I could see a beacon light,
Guiding me to my dear Savior,
And my rescue was in sight.

When by faith I sought forgiveness,
Turned my back on every sin,
In His mercy He forgave me,
And I was reborn again.

In His tender love and mercy,
I found safety in the storm,
For He paid the price at Calvary,
Now I'm safe within His arms.

From my life of aimless drifting,
To the harbor of His love,
Now the beacon light of Jesus,
Leads me to His throne above.

Gertrude B. McClain

Heavenly Dove

Sweet Holy Spirit
Sweet Heavenly Dove
May Your anointing spirit
bring peace from heaven above,
And for this peace we praise You
for giving us Your Son;
Now let Your Holy Spirit
descend on every one.
Descend, I pray, on me today
and fill my heart with love;
For everlasting joy and strength
comes only from above.

Paul L. Conklin

*And He saw the Spirit
of God coming down
in the form of a dove.*
Matthew 3:16